# STATE V. HARRIS

## SECOND EDITION
Case File

# STATE V. HARRIS

## SECOND EDITION
Case File

(A companion file to Fordyce v. Harris and Felson)

**Laurence M. Rose**
Professor of Law Emeritus
University of Miami
School of Law
Coral Gables, Florida

An adaptation of
Fordyce v. Harris and Felson
Originally written by
Abraham P. Ordover

NATIONAL INSTITUTE FOR TRIAL ADVOCACY

Address inquiries to:
Reprint Permission
National Institute for Trial Advocacy
1685 38th Street, Suite 200
Boulder, CO 80301-2735
Phone: (800) 225-6482
Fax: (720) 890-7069
E-mail: permissions@nita.org
ISBN 978-1-60156-169-5
FBA 1169
14 13 12 11    10 9 8 7 6 5 4 3 2 1
Printed in the United States of America

Official co-publisher of NITA.
WKLegaledu.com/NITA

# CONTENTS

# Acknowledgments

The original *State v. Harris* file was based on the *Fordyce v. Harris and Felson* file written by Abraham P. Ordover, one of the early authors of NITA case files and a former program director and faculty member. The passage of time and changes in case strategies have been addressed in these revisions, primarily to further the teaching goals and for skill development. This file is designed to be used in a trial advocacy program, either as skill exercises or a final trial, or both, and along with its companion, *Fordyce v. Harris and Felson*, can be effectively used to highlight the differences between civil and criminal advocacy techniques, as well as the effect of the different burdens of proof.

This file is dedicated to all of those who have contributed to the teaching of advocacy and the promotion of the profession.

LMR

# INTRODUCTION

The State of Nita has charged the defendant Gerald J. Harris with first degree assault with a deadly weapon.

The State alleges that on March 2, YR-1, Henry Fordyce was with a friend, Eva Marie Long, having a few drinks at Gus's Bar & Grill in Nita City. At about 11:00 p.m., Harris and Felson entered the bar and sat down at the next table. Fordyce claims that they began leering at Ms. Long and later made insulting remarks to her and Fordyce. A fight broke out; the police arrived and restored order. There were no serious injuries and no charges were brought.

Later that evening, according to the State, when Fordyce was on his way home and near an alley about fifty feet from the bar, he was attacked by the defendant and Felson. Harris allegedly hit him with a broom handle and Felson allegedly stomped on him with his boots.

Henry Fordyce was hospitalized with a fractured skull and has completely recovered. His medical bills were $37,000, and he lost wages of $28,000.

The defendant denies that he assaulted Fordyce. Harris says Fordyce was the aggressor in the bar, but contends he left right after the incident.

Reciprocal discovery, including the Grand Jury testimony, has been completed. The applicable law is contained in the proposed jury instructions set forth at the end of the case file.

All years in these materials are stated in the following form:

YR-0 indicates the actual year in which the case is being tried (i.e., the present year);
YR-1 indicates the next preceding year (please use the actual year);
YR-2 indicates the second preceding year (please use the actual year);
Earlier years are sequentially increased.

# SPECIAL INSTRUCTIONS FOR USE AS A FULL TRIAL

When this case file is used as the basis for a full trial, subject to the instructor's discretion, each side should call the listed four witnesses. If the instructor varies these instructions, the party listed below should select and prepare the witness.

State

    Henry Fordyce
    Eva Marie Long
    Peter Logan
    Edward Felson

Defense

    Melissa Angel
    Gerald Harris
    Glenda Barkan
    Ben Sanders

# STIPULATIONS

The parties have agreed to the following stipulations:

1.     In Nita City, at the time of the alleged incident, the *Late Movie* was one and one-half hours in length and was broadcast from 11:30 p.m. to 1:00 a.m.

2.     All documents contained in the case file are authentic.

3.     The hospital records were made and kept in the regular course of the hospital's business and satisfy all of the requirements of the business records exception to the hearsay rule.

4.     The records of the U. S. Department of the Interior were made and kept in the regular course of the department's business and satisfy all the requirements of the business records and public records exceptions to the hearsay rule.

# In the District Court
## of the County of Darrow
### State of Nita

| | | |
|---|---|---|
| STATE OF NITA | ) | |
| | ) | |
| v. | ) | FILE NO. Cr. 137-YR-0 |
| | ) | |
| GERALD J. HARRIS | ) | |

## Indictment

The Grand Jury, on its oath, hereby charges the Defendant, GERALD J. HARRIS, with the crime of First Degree Assault with a Deadly Weapon, a violation of Nita Revised Criminal Code Section 453.78, a felony punishable by a prison term of a minimum of twelve and a maximum of twenty-five years, to wit:

On or about March 2, YR-1, in the vicinity of 2847 Founders Blvd., Nita City, Nita, the Defendant, GERALD J. HARRIS, did feloniously with intent to cause serious bodily injury to another person, namely HENRY C. FORDYCE, strike HENRY C. FORDYCE with a bludgeon and cause HENRY C. FORDYCE to suffer substantial risk of death by virtue of a fractured skull in violation of the peace and dignity of the laws of the State of Nita.

A TRUE BILL

*Mick Thompson*

_____

Foreperson
Nita Grand Jury
November 3, YR-1

*Ronny Lowes*

_____

Nita County State Attorney
November 3, YR-1

# STATEMENT GIVEN TO POLICE BY EDWARD FELSON OCTOBER 10, YR-1

EDWARD FELSON, having been informed of his right to remain silent, his right to an attorney, and that his statements may be used against him, voluntarily gives the following statement:

My name is Edward W. Felson. I am twenty-eight years old. I am currently being held in the Nita City Jail on the charge of armed robbery (15–30 years) of a liquor store in Nita City in July YR-1. I didn't do it and my lawyer will prove it at trial.

Gerald Harris is a friend of mine from high school. I haven't really seen him except to say "hi" since then, except for the night we went out to a wrestling show and then to a bar. I know he's got a girlfriend, but I don't remember her name. I met her once a little while before Gerry and I went out, but she didn't seem very friendly. It was like she was too good for me or something.

On March 2, I was staying at the Eastern Motel and Taxi headquarters, where I sometimes worked. I called to meet Gerry at his office on Founders Boulevard in Nita City. Gerry had done pretty well for himself since high school and owned his own business. I was having a hard time finding a full-time job, so I looked him up. I got to his office at about 7:30 p.m. He was finishing up some work, so I just sat around and talked with him. I told him I needed a job and asked if he could help me out. He explained that he had cleaning contracts that didn't allow him to hire convicted felons, so I was out of luck. It seemed to me that Gerry could have made an exception for an old friend, but I guess he's gotten too big for his britches now that he's a fancy business man. Anyhow, he asked me if I wanted to go out to a wresting show. He called up his old lady and asked her to come along, but she didn't want to go, so we went to the wresting show at the Arena, which was about four blocks away.

After the match, Gerry asked me if I wanted to get a couple of beers on him. I figured if I couldn't get a job, I might as well get a few free beers, so I went along. We went to a joint called Gus's Bar & Grill on Founders Boulevard. It's a neighborhood bar, pretty dark, but with good music. I guess we got there just before 11:00 p.m. We went in the front door and up to the bar. Gerry started hitting on the bartender. She wasn't bad looking and Gerry was trying to get something going for when she got off work. Gerry thinks he's a ladies' man with all his fancy clothes and everything, but near as I can tell, he was making a fool of himself. The bartender must have bought his line though, because she said she'd meet him after work. While this was going on, we had a beer at the bar.

After Gerry got his promise from the lady, we moved to a table with two chairs in the back part of the bar. It was the one nearest the booths. I was sitting with my back to the bar and Gerry was facing the bar, still making eyes at the bartender. I looked to my right and saw a working girl I recognized. She usually was hustling guys out on Founders Boulevard. I was just telling Gerry about this when this guy who smelled like a damned distillery comes flying at me and knocks me off my chair. He also hit the table and spilled a beer on Gerry.

I got up and started mixing it up with him. He was obviously pretty drunk, but when he picked up a chair, I got a little scared. I don't care what anybody says, I never picked up a beer bottle and threatened anybody. Gerry must have been mad at the guy for spilling beer on him because he hit the drunk pretty hard in the stomach.

About that time, a cop came in and broke the thing up. He told us all to cool it and go on home, but first took our names and addresses.

The fight wasn't any big deal and no one was hurt. Anyway, I didn't want to hassle with the cops. Gerry said he would drive me home in his red Beamer. During the ride, Gerry was still bitching about getting a little beer on him. I told him something like he'd come a long way from high school when he'd have been happy about having a beer to spill. We got to the motel about 11:20, and I left him at the motel office, then went to my room, watched some TV, and went to sleep.

Two days later, I got busted by the cops at my motel. They said I was under arrest for knocking the drunk from the bar upside the head. I told them I didn't have anything to do with it. They searched my room and asked if I had any boots. I told them I don't own any boots.

The next day, they put me in a lineup with Gerry and five other guys. They put me on $5,000 bail. I couldn't make it and big shot Gerry wouldn't go bail for me, so I stayed there for two weeks. Then we went to court, and I got a public defender. She got the case dismissed, and they let me go. I now know the drunk in the bar is named Fordyce, but I never did nothing to him.

# Grand Jury Testimony of Eva Marie Long*
## November 3, YR-1

1    My name is Eva Marie Long. I'm twenty-five years old. My address is 676 28th Street, Apartment
2    11B. I've lived at that address for four years. I'm a freelance photographer and model.

3    I was born in Racine, Wisconsin, and went to public schools there until my family moved to
4    Montrose, Nita. I finished high school at Montrose High and went on to Nita State. I got an AB
5    in art history in YR-4.

6    I first met Henry Fordyce when I was a sophomore in college. Over the next three years we
7    dated occasionally, but mainly we were friends. After college we sent each other Christmas cards and
8    ran into each other once or twice, but never dated.

9    I was pleasantly surprised when Henry called me in late February. I can't remember the date,
10    but I do remember he said he was in town for some kind of forest rangers' convention and that he
11    had plenty of time and didn't have to work too hard. We made a date for March 2, which was the
12    first night I was free.

13    He came by my apartment at about 10:00 p.m. I was surprised that he was so late; he said he
14    would be there around 9:00. He said he'd been drinking with some friends at a local bar and had
15    lost track of the time. He looked loaded, so I asked him how many he'd had. He said, "One or two
16    scotches." My guess is it was more like five or six.

17    We stayed at my place for a few minutes, but then left for Gus's Bar & Grill, which is around
18    the corner. I'd say we got there at about 10:15 p.m., but I'm not positive as to the time.

19    Gus's was quiet, as usual. That's what I like about it. We sat down at a table that was two tables
20    away from the door. Henry ordered a scotch for himself and a vodka tonic for me. We talked and
21    drank for about forty-five minutes and had just started our second round when some guys came
22    over and sat down two tables over, the one farthest away from the door.

23    The guys at that table hadn't been there five minutes when they started making really awful
24    comments about me. I got angry and told one, who I later found out was Harris, to knock it off.
25    Then the other guy yelled out to Henry that I'm a prostitute. I think he actually said "hooker."

26    That was it. I was in tears. Henry got up and started over toward them. Felson grabbed a beer
27    bottle by the neck. He told Henry if he came one step closer he'd cut his face off. I tried to help
28    Henry, but one of them threw me to the ground. It's all so confused now.

29    I stayed on the floor until the police came. It seems everyone in the place was either in the
30    fight or trying to break it up. The only thing I'm sure of is that at one point Harris knocked Henry

---

\*   The transcript of Long's Grand Jury testimony was excerpted so that only her answers are reprinted here. Assume that this is a true and accurate rendering of those answers.

1   down with a punch. One other thing: I did hear Harris and Felson screaming to each other. One of

2   them—I couldn't tell which—said, "Kill him."

3       A cop arrived and broke things up. He took all our names and addresses, and asked what hap-

4   pened. After a while, he told us he wasn't going to make an arrest and that we should all go home.

5   We left about five minutes after Harris and Felson.

6       When we left the bar, and before we were even a block away, Harris and Felson jumped out of

7   an alley and clobbered us. I was really startled when they jumped out. The alley was dark, so they

8   just came from nowhere. Harris threw me to the ground. As I was on the ground, I was to Harris's

9   right. He was facing the street, and Henry was facing the alley. Harris had a small pole of some kind,

10   it looked like a broomstick, in his right hand. He hit Henry over the head with it. Henry went down

11   and then Felson started kicking him. The whole time I could see Harris's right profile. I guess it

12   was about five to ten seconds before I started screaming, got up, and ran for help. It was then I saw

13   Felson standing to Harris's left.

14       When I came back with a cop, Henry was out cold and all bloodied. Harris and Felson were

15   nowhere to be seen. When the ambulance came, I got in with Henry and the cop followed in his

16   car. On the way to the hospital Henry woke up. He said his head was really hurting and that Felson

17   and Harris had nearly killed him and that they would pay for it.

18       At the hospital, I told the police what had happened. A few days later, Officer Logan called me

19   to come down to the police station. I picked Felson and Harris out of a lineup. I knew right when I

20   saw them they were the ones. I later told the police, however, that I couldn't be sure what Felson ac-

21   tually did to Henry. I understand they dropped the charges against both of them. I don't know why.

22       I have had some problems with drugs, but that was all in the past. I was arrested twice for hav-

23   ing cocaine. Both times the charges were dismissed. The first time it was because the person who

24   actually owned the stuff confessed. The second time the cops lost the evidence. That stuff was a

25   friend's, not mine. The most recent thing was a couple of months ago. I tried using some cocaine,

26   and there must have been something in it because it knocked me right out. They took me to the

27   hospital where they gave me a shot of something and let me go home. The police did question me,

28   but there were no charges. That last incident scared me. After that last time, I learned differently. I

29   stopped using it then and haven't used any since.

# GRAND JURY TESTIMONY OF GERALD HARRIS*
## NOVEMBER 3, YR-1

1    My name is Gerald J. Harris. I am twenty-seven years old. I live at 24 Wilson Street in Glendale,
2    Nita. Glendale is a suburb of Nita City. I currently own Sanders Cleaning Services, Inc. Our office
3    and warehouse are located at 2608 Founders Boulevard in Nita City. I had gotten in trouble some
4    when I was a kid, but got straightened out by my former boss, Ben Sanders. I started working for
5    Mr. Sanders right out of high school, and I bought the business from him in YR-3 when he retired.
6    My business does contract cleaning services for various businesses and governmental agencies.
7        I recently had some business trouble with some political hacks in the Nita City municipal gov-
8    ernment. They made some claims that I had been overcharging for the services I perform for the
9    city, but their allegations are totally unfounded. It's all been cleared up now. The business is going
10   very well. I employ over one hundred people and last year the business grossed $2,000,000. You
11   don't make that kind of money by overcharging the city, or anyone else for that matter. That kind
12   of reputation can kill you in this business.
13       I am single, but have a steady girlfriend. Her name is Glenda Barkan. She lives in Apartment 22
14   at 522 Grace Avenue in Nita City.
15       On March 2, I got a call at work from an old high-school friend of mine, Eddie Felson. I hadn't
16   spent any time with Eddie since high school, although I'd see him around from time to time. He
17   said he was staying at the Eastern Motel, and he asked if we could get together that night, so I ar-
18   ranged for him to meet me at the office at about 7:30 p.m. I was working late that night, as I do
19   most every night, being that I'm the CEO for my business.
20       Eddie showed up a little early, and we sat around and talked for a while. He was looking for a
21   job, so we talked about what he'd been up to for the past couple of years. It turned out that he'd had
22   some trouble with the law and was convicted of a couple of crimes. I told him that unfortunately,
23   given the fact that I had a number of cleaning contracts with the state, local, and federal govern-
24   ments, I wasn't allowed to have any convicted felons on my staff. He seemed a little disappointed,
25   but said that he understood.
26       I suggested we go out and see a wrestling match at the Arena, a few blocks away. I called Glenda,
27   but she said she had some work to do and told me to come over later that evening. She had met
28   Eddie once before, but he seemed to rub her the wrong way. We went to the Arena, and saw three
29   to four matches. I didn't care for the wrestling, but Eddie seemed to really get off on the fights and
30   chair slamming. We left a little after 10:30 p.m., and we decided to go down to Gus's Bar & Grill,

---

*    The transcript of Harris's Grand Jury testimony was excerpted so that only his answers are reprinted here. Assume that this is
a true and accurate rendering of those answers.

1 which is about a block away from my office. I felt bad about not being able to help Eddie out with
2 a job, so I figured the least I could do was take him out for beer.

3     We got to Gus's at about 10:45 p.m. or so. Even though it's only about a block from my office,
4 I really don't hang out there. I had been there only a couple of times before. It's a little bit of a dive,
5 always dark and smelly. When we got to Gus's, we went up to the bar to order a couple of beers.
6 The barmaid there was kind of cute, and I was kidding her about taking her out sometime. I think
7 I asked her what time she got off work and whether she would go out with me, but I was only jok-
8 ing. It was just talk and she knew it. As I said, I had a date to meet my girlfriend later that night.

9     We had a beer at the bar and then took our second to a table. There were four tables with two
10 chairs in the room, and we went to the one all the way in the back of the room. I was sitting facing
11 the bar, and Eddie was sitting with his back to the bar.

12     We looked over, and one table away was a really good looking woman and a guy who looked like
13 he was smashed. Eddie told me she was a hooker. He started giving her the eye when all of a sud-
14 den the drunk, who I now know to be Fordyce, comes flying across the room and knocks Eddie to
15 the floor. He also hit our table and spilled some beer on me, but it was no big deal. I went after the
16 drunk just to break up the fight. The woman was involved somehow, but I just pushed her aside. I
17 never saw Eddie with a beer bottle in his hand, but it all happened so quick, he could have had one.

18     We were wrestling around on the floor when a cop came in and broke up the fight. He told us
19 to take it easy and just go home, but first took our names and addresses. To tell you the truth, I was
20 glad he said that, because it was pretty clear to me that Eddie had changed a whole lot since high
21 school, and I really didn't want to have anything to do with him.

22     I agreed to drive Eddie back to his motel. The drunk and the woman were still in the bar.
23 During the ride, Eddie said something like, "I'll teach that guy to beat on me." I told him he should
24 cool it, that the guy was just a drunk and nobody got hurt, so he should just forget it.

25     We got to his motel about 11:30, and I left him at the motel office. I then went back to my
26 office and cleaned up a couple of things and then drove over to Glenda's. It's located about twenty
27 blocks from my office, about two miles away. I got there about midnight. I guess Glenda was sleep-
28 ing when I got to her apartment because it took her a couple of minutes to answer the door. I would
29 have left, but I heard the TV, so I just waited until she answered the door.

30     We sat around for about an hour until the end of the *Late Movie* and then I went home. I told
31 Glenda about the fight in the bar. She was real upset with me and told me I should grow up. She
32 said something like, "Just because you went out with a friend from high school doesn't mean you
33 have to act like you're still in high school." I told her that I felt sorry for Eddie, but that I guessed
34 she was right about him being a bad apple. I got home at about 1:30 a.m. You can make pretty good
35 time to Glendale when there's no traffic.

1     A couple of days later, I got picked up by the cops. They told me that Fordyce, the drunk from

2    Gus's, got beat up outside the bar. I didn't say anything to them about it, but I wasn't too surprised

3    because he was a drunk looking to get into a fight. The cops put Eddie and me in a lineup. They

4    charged me with assault or something like that and made me post a bond of $5,000 and threatened

5    me with twelve to twenty-five years. A couple of weeks later, I went down to court with my lawyer,

6    and the DA dropped the charges against me. The worst part of the whole thing was that Glenda

7    was so upset.

8     Just like I told the cops, I didn't have anything to do with beating up this Fordyce guy. The first

9    and only time I saw him was in Gus's on March 2. I feel sorry for the guy, but I'm not going to pay

10   for something I didn't do.

# GRAND JURY TESTIMONY OF PETER LOGAN*
## NOVEMBER 3, YR-1

1    My name is Peter C. Logan. I live at 4281 Oceanside Drive in Nita City. My wife teaches at

2    Nita East Elementary School, and we have two children. Debbie is eight and Richard is four. I'm

3    thirty-four years old and have an associate degree in police sciences from Nita Community College.

4    I got out of school when I was twenty, in YR-14. I served three years in the Marines and was

5    honorably discharged in YR-11. After that I worked for several years in my father-in-law's business,

6    a chain of dry cleaning stores. I started as a clerk, then moved up to manager of the central plant

7    where they do all the actual cleaning, when I realized I just wasn't happy being in that business and

8    really wanted to be a police officer. Being a cop was something I'd wanted to do ever since I was a

9    child. My uncle was a police officer, so I think that's where I got the idea.

10    I started at the Nita City Police Academy in YR-6. It was a six-month program, and I finished

11    first in my class. Since then I have been a patrolman, and I have just taken the sergeant's exam. I

12    scored higher than anyone else and will get the first opening, which should be in six to ten months.

13    On the night of March 2, I was assigned to foot patrol in the area of Gus's Bar. It's a high crime

14    area, and I was part of a special high visibility unit that had been assigned to the area for several

15    months. At 11:00 p.m., I was alerted to a 911 call about a fight in Gus's Bar. I was only a block

16    away. I ran there and entered the bar and found three men going at it. A fourth person, a woman,

17    appeared to be caught in the middle and was hiding under a nearby table. I broke up the fight, sepa-

18    rated the people, and took all their names. No one seemed sure how it had happened, and despite

19    some overturned chairs, there wasn't any real damage. I gave them all a warning and told them to

20    go home. I did not issue any citations or arrest anyone.

21    When I was on my next loop around the neighborhood heading south on Founders near Gus's

22    at 11:35 p.m., I heard screaming and again encountered the woman who had been under the table.

23    Her name is Eva Marie Long. She came running towards me yelling. I couldn't make out every-

24    thing she was saying, but I did hear her say, "They're killing my friend." I drew my weapon and ran

25    toward the alley she was pointing to. When I got there Henry Fordyce was out cold and bleeding

26    badly from his head. I called for an ambulance and a backup unit.

27    When the Memorial Hospital ambulance arrived, I helped them load Fordyce inside. The wom-

28    an got in with him. Long told me that a stick was used as a weapon. I searched the vicinity of the

---

\*    The transcript of Logan's Grand Jury testimony was excerpted so that only his answers are reprinted here. Assume that this is a
true and accurate rendering of those answers.

1 alley and did not find a stick or other weapons. I followed in the backup vehicle, which had arrived
2 about the same time as the ambulance.

3     At the hospital, Long told me she and Fordyce had been attacked by the same men who had
4 been in the fight at the bar. When the doctors let me talk to Fordyce, he confirmed her identifica-
5 tions, but he was awfully groggy at the time. I put out a BOLO on Felson and Harris.

6     A couple of days later, when they were both under arrest, I scheduled a lineup for Ms. Long.
7 Fordyce was still in the hospital and couldn't participate. She immediately picked out both men.
8 However, the detectives' and my later conversations with her indicated she was positive of the Harris
9 ID, but much less sure on Felson. My investigation revealed that Harris had a good alibi, and with
10 the weakness of her ID and the fact that Fordyce probably didn't see much—the alley where I found
11 him was very dark—I recommended that the charges be dismissed. They were.

12     I found out that Felson was later arrested for a July 10, YR-1, liquor store robbery. I spoke with
13 him regarding his involvement in the Fordyce matter, and he denied everything. As part of the plea
14 negotiations on the liquor store case, he agreed to tell the truth. The State's Attorney agreed to the
15 deal. Felson pleaded to the liquor store charge and agreed to testify before the Grand Jury.

# GRAND JURY TESTIMONY OF GLENDA BARKAN*
## NOVEMBER 3, YR-1

1     My name is Glenda Barkan. I am twenty-two years old and single. I live in Apartment 22 at
2  522 Grace Avenue in Nita City. I am a senior at Nita University, majoring in history. I'll graduate
3  in June of this year and hope to go on to law school. My boyfriend is Gerald Harris. We have been
4  seeing each other for over a year. Gerald owns a cleaning business called Sanders Cleaning Services,
5  Inc. I guess he does pretty well in the business, but we really don't talk about his work much. He's
6  more interested in what I do at school, probably because he never got a chance to go to college.
7  Depending on where I get into law school, we'll probably get married in a year or so if our relation-
8  ship stays as good as it's been.
9     On March 2, I got a phone call from Gerald at about 7:00 p.m. He was supposed to come
10  over to my apartment that night to watch some TV or listen to music—nothing special, we were
11  just going to spend some time together. He called me to tell me that he was meeting a friend of his
12  named Eddie Felson. Gerald wanted me to go to a wrestling match with him and Felson, but I told
13  him that I had some studying to do, so I would pass. Gerald and I had met Felson one time before
14  and I thought he was a jerk, but Gerald seemed to like him. Gerald told me they had been friends
15  in high school, but he hadn't spent any time with him since then. I was a little upset that Gerald
16  was standing me up, but because I did need to do some reading, I told him to come by when he
17  finished with Felson.
18     I finished reading my assignment and turned on the television to catch the 11:00 p.m. news. I
19  must have fallen asleep, because a little later I was awakened by the doorbell. It was Gerald. I don't
20  remember what time it was, but the *Late Movie* was on when Gerald woke me up. He came in and
21  we talked for a while. He seemed a little upset, so I asked him what was the matter. Gerald told me
22  that Felson had gotten in a fight at some bar over a girl and that he had to break it up. It couldn't
23  have been too serious because he wasn't disheveled or bruised at all. I told Gerald that he really
24  should grow up. I don't believe in fighting for any reason, especially a bar fight over some girl.
25     Gerald stayed for a while and we talked. The TV was still on, although the volume was way
26  down. I think he left at about 1:00 a.m. because the *Late Movie* had just ended.
27     A couple of days later, Gerald called me and came over. He told me that I was right about Felson,
28  because the guy Felson was fighting got beat up pretty bad and Gerald suspected that Felson did
29  it. He said that he and Felson got arrested that afternoon. I was really upset about the whole thing.
30  Gerald calmed me down and told me not to worry, that he wasn't involved. It turned out all right

---

\*   The transcript of Barkan's Grand Jury testimony was excerpted so that only her answers are reprinted here. Assume that this is
a true and accurate rendering of those answers.

1  because the charges were dropped against Gerald. I just hope Gerald has learned his lesson about
2  the kinds of people he should hang out with. I'm sure he had nothing to do with beating up poor
3  Mr. Fordyce. He's just not that kind of man. If he was, I wouldn't have anything to do with him.

# GRAND JURY TESTIMONY OF MELISSA ANGEL*
## NOVEMBER 3, YR-1

1    My name is Melissa Angel. I am twenty-seven years old and divorced. I have no kids. I live at

2    3056 Jackson Avenue, Apartment 3B, in Nita City. I'm a bartender at Gus's Bar & Grill at 2847

3    Founders Boulevard in Nita City. Gus's is a small bar that serves food. It's got typical low bar light-

4    ing. The music is kept pretty soft for a bar. I've been working there for the past five years.

5    On March 2, I was working the night shift, from 4:00 p.m. until midnight. It was a pretty slow

6    night. At about 11:00 p.m., two guys came in and sat at the bar. I later found out they were Gerald

7    Harris and Eddie Felson. They both ordered beers. Harris was all "Mr. Cool" and trying to flirt

8    with me and kept asking me when I got off work. He was being a real pest. I knew he was probably

9    all talk, but partially to shut him up and partially because he wasn't bad looking, I agreed to go out

10    with him when I got off work at midnight. The other guy, Felson, wasn't saying much, just drink-

11    ing his beer. The two had a beer at the bar and then took another and moved to a table towards the

12    back.

13    A couple of minutes later I came out of the kitchen and a fight had started. It was Harris and

14    Felson wrestling with a guy who had been sitting with a girl at another table. They were fighting

15    near the table where Felson and Harris had been sitting. I don't know how the fight started, but it

16    seemed like Harris was doing a number on the other guy. The cook must have called 911, and a

17    cop—I think his name was Logan—came in and broke up the fight. He didn't arrest anyone, just

18    took their names and told them to leave.

19    Harris and Felson left the bar at around 11:20. Fordyce and Ms. Long left about ten minutes

20    later. I went back to work. A few minutes later, I heard screaming from outside, ran to the door, and

21    saw Long and Fordyce in the alley. Logan must have called for an ambulance and a backup police

22    unit. The ambulance got there almost immediately. Logan told me that Fordyce got beat up.

23    At midnight, when we closed, Harris had not come back to the bar, so I figured he'd forgotten

24    me and I left. I left a couple of minutes after twelve. I started walking down the block when I saw a

25    red car with a guy I thought was Harris driving north in front of Gus's down Founders Boulevard.

26    I called out to him, but he did not turn or stop. I don't know if anyone else was in the car. I never

27    saw Harris again.

---

\*    The transcript of Angel's Grand Jury testimony was excerpted so that only her answers are reprinted here. Assume that this is a true and accurate rendering of those answers.

# GRAND JURY TESTIMONY OF MELISSA ANGEL

## NOVEMBER 3, YR-1

# GRAND JURY TESTIMONY OF HENRY FORDYCE*
## NOVEMBER 3, YR-1

1     My name is Henry C. Fordyce. I was born on August 18, YR-25, in Nita City, Nita. My legal
2     residence is with my parents at 1421 Seminole Drive here in Nita City, but I work for the U.S.
3     Department of the Interior as a forest ranger at Bear Lake National Forest in the western part of
4     Nita. I work twenty days on and get off for five. Most times I come home on my days off.

5     I went to the Nita public schools and graduated from Central High in YR-8. I was really inter-
6     ested in biology and the environment. I decided to attend Nita State University in Montrose to try
7     to get a combined degree in forestry and environmental sciences. It's a special program they have.
8     I graduated in YR-4 and have been working as a forest ranger since then. My current position is
9     Senior Forest Ranger. My annual salary is $84,000 plus benefits.

10    One of my special interests is resource administration and, in February, I was able to get the
11    department to send me to Nita City to attend a month-long seminar on that subject, which was
12    being held at Nita City College. The dates of the seminar were February 11 to March 15. I attended
13    classes all day and was living at home with my parents.

14    Eva Marie Long is a woman I dated in college. We still see each other socially from time to time
15    when I'm in Nita City. I called her when I first got into town, and on March 2, I went over to her
16    apartment at about 9:45 p.m. I had been at Fenster's Bar with some friends before then because
17    Eva said she wouldn't be ready until 10:00 p.m. I had two scotches at Fenster's and watched a pro
18    basketball game on TV.

19    Eva and I talked for a while at her apartment, and then she suggested we go have a drink at
20    Gus's, which is a bar near her apartment. I think it is actually called Gus's Bar & Grill. We got there
21    about 10:30 p.m.

22    It was really very nice. The music was low enough so we could talk, and we were discussing old
23    times. I hadn't seen her in several months, and it was good to be together again.

24    We were seated at the second table in from the door. I was facing the bar and Eva had her back
25    to the bar and the door. We ordered a couple of drinks.

26    I noticed two really tough-looking guys at about 11:00 p.m. They walked behind Eva, so she
27    couldn't see that they were staring at her. They sat down at the last table from the door, two tables
28    away from us. No one was at the table in between. I didn't recognize either of them and Eva didn't
29    appear to either.

---

\*    The transcript of Fordyce's Grand Jury testimony was excerpted so that only his answers are reprinted here. Assume that this is
a true and accurate rendering of those answers.

1    A few minutes later, the one who I now know is Harris started leering and ogling at Eva. This
2  time she saw it and was upset. I told Harris to knock it off. He laughed at me and poked the other
3  guy, who I now know is Felson. The two of them really started getting on Eva. I can't remember
4  everything they said, but I remember Harris saying, "Hey honey, drop that stiff and come over
5  here. I'll show you a real good time." I particularly didn't like the way he said "real." Then Felson, I
6  remember this too, said, "I remember you from down on the corner. What's the matter—business
7  bad—too many cops around?"

8    Eva Marie started to cry. I was really angry. I went over and grabbed Felson by his shirt, on either
9  side of his neck, and shook him. He fell off his chair, got up, grabbed a beer bottle, and came after
10 me. I dodged his first swing and picked up a chair to protect myself. When he came at me a second
11 time, I used the chair to keep him away. I never hit Felson with the chair. While I was still holding
12 the chair and before I could get it in position to protect myself, Harris punched me in the gut from
13 the other side, and I doubled over. The wind was knocked out of me and I was dizzy. Before they
14 could jump on me and really do some damage, the cop came and broke up the fight. His name was
15 Logan.

16   Logan took everybody's name and asked what had happened. When it was all over, he told us
17 he wasn't going to press charges and to go home. I couldn't believe he didn't arrest those guys for
18 what they did.

19   Felson and Harris got up and left. I was still a little dazed, so Eva and I stayed around for a few
20 minutes.

21   It was about 11:35 p.m. when we left. We walked out the front door, turned left, and walked
22 up Founders Boulevard towards 28th Street. I was walking on the curb side and Eva was on my left.

23   We had only gone about fifty feet from the bar when Harris jumped out of a dark alley. He
24 had a broom handle, or that's what it looked like, raised over his head. He knocked Eva Marie over
25 with his body as he jumped out, pulled me into the alley, and clobbered me on my head. I went
26 down and was flat on my back. At this point, I was facing down the alley and he was standing over
27 me, facing the street. The pain was unbelievable. Then Harris hit me with the broom handle again.
28 Things were getting gray, but I remember seeing Felson come over from my right. I felt him stomp
29 on my stomach with his boot, once, then again. Then I finally passed out.

30   The next thing I remember I was in the ambulance on the way to the hospital. Eva was with me.
31 She said, "You could have been killed. You shouldn't have tried to protect me in the bar."

32   At the hospital they told me my skull was fractured, but I was lucky and probably wouldn't have
33 any brain damage. I stayed in the hospital, and they ran every test in the book over the next two
34 weeks. Blood samples, urine samples, CT scans; they never let up. All night long they woke me up
35 to take my pulse and temperature and make sure I wasn't in a coma. Finally, after two weeks, they
36 let me go home, but the doctor wouldn't let me go back to work for four months.

1    The terrible throbbing pain went away after about a week. While I had it, they gave me all sorts
2    of pain killers, things I'd never heard of, but they didn't do any good. It finally just got better. The
3    dizziness and nausea, however, lasted for almost four months. All they gave me for that was a little
4    Compazine and some Darvocet, and they only helped a little.

5    My doctor said because of the nature of my work that I couldn't go back on the job until I had
6    no dizziness for two weeks. I went back to work in early July.

7    My salary was $7,000 a month gross, and I missed four months. I was paid for one month be-
8    cause I had two weeks of sick leave and two weeks of vacation coming. I don't remember the exact
9    amounts of my hospital and drug bills, but they were over $37,000.

10   No one ever called me about the dropping of the original charges, but I am pleased the State's
11   Attorney is seeking an indictment now.

12   I have been arrested a couple of times, but I have never been convicted of anything more than
13   speeding. The arrests were about three months apart and both were in Wolf Creek, Nita, which is
14   not too far from Bear Lake Park, where I work. Sometimes, when I have some time off, I go there
15   instead of coming home to see my parents. The first arrest was when the police came to a party that
16   one of the other rangers had. They came a couple of times and asked us to hold it down. On the
17   third trip back, they came and took us all downtown and arrested everyone. We all stayed in jail
18   overnight, and the next day the charges were dismissed.

19   The second arrest was in a bar in Wolf Creek. I had had too much to drink. We had been help-
20   ing fight a forest fire for two weeks. We had just gotten it under control, and this was my first night
21   off. When the cop came in and told me I'd had enough and ought to go home, I cussed him out
22   pretty badly—or at least that's what the people who were with me say. Frankly, I don't remember
23   any of it. Anyway, the cop says I grabbed him by his uniform while I was doing that. I got a lawyer
24   and the charges were dropped. Apparently the police officer was pretty reasonable about it.

25   I got into an argument with Frank Allen, another ranger, about a year ago. He and I had been
26   dating the same waitress at the park's restaurant. He told me not to see her again. I told him that it
27   was not his business to tell her who to see and that as long as she still wanted to see me, I was going
28   to go out with her. There was a little pushing and shoving. No one got hurt and he later apologized.

29   I have brought with me the bills you requested. The first is the statement from Memorial
30   Hospital (see Exhibit A). And there are bills from Dr. Stern (see Exhibit B) and Dr. Hampton (see
31   Exhibit C) and one from Robineau's Pharmacy (see Exhibit D).

# GRAND JURY TESTIMONY OF EDWARD FELSON*
## NOVEMBER 3, YR-1

1  My name is Edward Felson, and I swear to tell the truth. I am currently incarcerated in the Nita
2  City Jail, and I am charged with the crime of armed robbery of a liquor store on July 10, YR-1.

3      I have agreed to and have pleaded guilty according to a plea bargain I made. The deal is this: I
4  will plead guilty to misdemeanor attempted robbery and will receive a sentence of 364 days. I know
5  I could have received a sentence of fifteen years minimum on the armed robbery charge. I also have
6  agreed to tell the truth in the case against Gerry Harris, and I will not be charged with anything in
7  the Fordyce matter. I could have been charged with first degree assault with a deadly weapon and
8  sentenced to twelve to twenty-five years on the Fordyce thing.

9      The truth is this: after we left the bar, Gerry and I walked over to his red BMW and started
10 to drive away. Gerry was really ticked off at this Fordyce guy for starting the fight, spilling beer on
11 Gerry, and beginning the hassle with the cops. Gerry said that he wanted to show the guy a lesson,
12 so why don't we jump him when he gets out of the bar. I really didn't want to do it, but Gerry said
13 that he might be able to get me job or give me a loan, so I said OK. We drove around to the back
14 of the bar and parked in the alley. We walked down the alley towards the bar. I found a broomstick
15 lying in the alley and I gave it to Gerry.

16     When this Fordyce guy came near the alley, Gerry jumped out of the alley and hit him in the
17 head. I figured I had to do something, so I kicked the guy in the stomach and ran. I heard Gerry say
18 "You deserve this, you punk," and then he caught up with me. He threw the stick in a dumpster.
19 We jumped into his car and drove away.

20     Gerry told me to keep my mouth shut and he'd make it up to me. He said he really smacked
21 the guy in the head hard and knew he got him good. He drove me to my motel, and we said our
22 goodbyes. He never called and he never helped me.

23     When the police arrested me, I lied because of my record and I knew Gerry wouldn't talk. I
24 would have never told the truth except for this plea bargain, but it is the truth.

---

\*    The transcript of Felson's Grand Jury testimony was excerpted so that only his answers are reprinted here. Assume that this is a true and accurate rendering of those answers.

# MEMORIAL HOSPITAL
## NITA CITY, NITA 99997

### STATEMENT OF ACCOUNT
### APRIL 4, YR-1

*Patient:*     Henry C. Fordyce
1421 Seminole Dr.
Nita City, Nita 99990

| | |
|---|---|
| Emergency Room (3/2/YR-1) | $  1,900.00 |
| Private Room Charge (3/3–3/17/YR-1) | $ 15,475.00 |
| Radiology Consultation | $     927.50 |
| X-rays | $  1,425.00 |
| Laboratory | $  2,137.50 |
| Pharmacy | $  1,020.00 |
| Radiology (CT Scan) (3/3/YR-1) | $     940.00 |
| Attending Physicians | $  2,580.00 |
| Private Nursing Services | $  2,275.00 |
| **TOTAL** | **$28,680.00** |

# John Stern, MD, FACS, PC
## 2211 Smith Boulevard, Nita City, Nita 99995

TO:      **Mr. Henry C. Fordyce**       **DATE:**     **3/21/YR-1**
                **1421 Seminole Drive**
                **Nita City, Nita 99990**

**Statement for Professional Services**

      **Treatment for head injuries**
      **March 3 – March 17, YR-1**            **$6,400.00**

# John Stern, MD, FACS, PC
2011 Smith Boulevard, Nile City, Nute 99995

TO: Ms. Irene C. Porter      DATE:      3/2/YR-1
1211 Sea Front Drive
Nile City, Nile 99090

Statement for Professional Services

Evaluation for knee injuries
March 2 – March 7, YR-1                              $6,400.00

**Exhibit C**

# WARREN HAMPTON, MD
### FAMILY PRACTICE
*1061 E. Walnut Street*
*Nita City, Nita 99994*

May 2, YR-1

TO:  Mr. Henry C. Fordyce
    1421 Seminole Drive
    Nita City, Nita 99990

For Medical Services Rendered        $1720.00

# WARREN HAMPTON, MD
### FAMILY PRACTICE
100 E. Walnut Street
Vine City, Ohio 99909

May 2, 19-1

To: Mr. Henry C. Ford, Sr.
1123 Seminole Drive
Port Charles, Ohio 99906

For Medical Services Rendered .......... $1,720.00

# Robineau's Pharmacy
## 2810 North Main Street Nita City, Nita 99991

July 25, YR-1

**Statement of Account for:**                                   Mr. Henry C. Fordyce
1421 Seminole Drive
Nita City, Nita 99990

For prescriptions filled between March 17, YR-1, and June 3, YR-1.              $480.00

**TOTAL DUE:**                                                      **$480.00**

## PAST DUE
*Please give this matter your prompt attention.*

**Exhibit 1**

# MEMORIAL HOSPITAL
## Nita City, Nita 99997

PATIENT:   Henry C. Fordyce          DOB:          August 18, YR-25
           1421 Seminole Dr.
           Nita City, Nita 99990

EMPLOYER: U.S. Dept. of Interior     NOK:          Mrs. Stephen Fordyce
          Forest Service                           Same Address
          Regional Office
          Nita City, Nita 99998

INSURANCE: Gov't Policy  Plan 3/80

ADMITTED: 3/2/YR-1 11:50 p.m.

| | |
|---|---|
| 3/2/YR-1<br>11:50 p.m. | ER patient arrived via ambulance. Patient reports having been unconscious briefly after being hit over head with broom handle. Also reports being kicked several times in abdomen. Bleeding from scalp, nose, and ears. Tender in lower right quad. Multiple bruises abdomen and pelvic area. B.P. 150/100. Resp. 20. Temp. 98.2. Pulse 100. Blood alcohol level .15%. Typed and cross matched. Full skull and abdomen series and CAT scan (brain) ordered stat. |

R. Jones, MD

| | |
|---|---|
| 3/3/YR-1<br>12:35 a.m. | Skull and abdominal series as per Jones's order. Skull positive, hairline fracture left skull 3 mm. above ear socket. Fracture extends 4 mm diagonally toward left temple. Abdominal negative. CT scan for brain negative. |

A. Lassiter, Technician

| | |
|---|---|
| 3/3/YR-1<br>8:20 a.m. | Patient awake complains of restless night, little sleep, sharp pains in area of fractures, general pain in abdominal area. B.P. 120/80, Pulse 80, Resp. 22, Temp. 98.4, Morphine IV |

J. Stern, MD

| | |
|---|---|
| 3/3/YR-1<br>10:30 a.m. | Patient complains of headache, disequilibrium, and abdominal ache. Continue IV Morphine. |

F. X. Smith, MD

| | |
|---|---|
| 3/3/YR-1<br>1:00 p.m. | Patient semi-comatose. Discontinue Morphine IV Complains of severe sharp pain in skull. B.P. 140/90, Resp. 20, Temp. 100.2, Pulse 88. |

J. Stern, MD

| | |
|---|---|
| 3/3/YR-1<br>6:00 p.m. | No new orders. Patient stable. |

J. Stern, MD

| | |
|---|---|
| 3/4/YR-1<br>12:30 a.m. | Patient awake. Complains of pain in skull area. Resume Morphine IV. |

L. Pringle, MD

| | |
|---|---|
| 3/4/YR-1<br>7:00 a.m. | Patient pain less. Reduce Morphine. Patient awake, alert. Pupils normal. Not to leave bed. B.P. 120/80. |

J. Stern, MD

| | |
|---|---|
| 3/4/YR-1<br>4:00 p.m. | Some improvement noted. Continue Morphine overnight if needed. |

J. Stern, MD

| | |
|---|---|
| 3/5/YR-1<br>7:00 a.m. | Continued improvement. Progress good. Discontinue Morphine. Darvocet as needed. |

J. Stern, MD

| | |
|---|---|
| 3/5/YR-1<br>4:30 p.m. | No new orders. |

J. Stern. MD

| | |
|---|---|
| 3/6/YR-1<br>7:30 a.m. | Patient may leave bed within room. Discontinue if any loss of balance. |

J. Stern, MD

| | |
|---|---|
| 3/7/YR-1<br>8:00 a.m. | Patient staggers when walking but only slightly. Continue moving about room. |

W. Russell, MD

| | |
|---|---|
| 3/8/YR-1<br>8:15 a.m. | Less staggering. Still complains of sharp head pain. Continue Darvocet. |

J. Stern, MD

| | |
|---|---|
| 3/9/YR-1<br>7:00 a.m. | Patient may take light exercise and resume normal diet. |

J. Stern, MD

| | |
|---|---|
| 3/10/YR-1<br>8:30 a.m. | X-ray report satisfactory. |

J. Stern, MD

| | |
|---|---|
| 3/11/YR-1<br>11:20 a.m. | Ophthalmological work-up. Some distortion at margins. Should clear up in a few more days. |

J. Ferris, MD

| | |
|---|---|
| 3/12/YR-1<br>8:20 p.m. | Some dizziness reported by Nurse Quigley. Compazine as needed. |
| | B. Abrams, MD |
| 3/13/YR-1<br>8:00 p.m. | Dizziness persists with some headaches. Compazine and Darvocet as needed. |
| | J. Stern, MD |
| 3/14/YR-1<br>7:30 a.m. | Resting comfortably. No new instructions. |
| | J. Stern, MD |
| 3/14/YR-1<br>7:45 p.m. | X-ray report shows satisfactory healing. Dizziness persists. |
| | J. Stern, MD |
| 3/15/YR-1<br>4:30 p.m. | Ophthalmology tests show vision normal. |
| | J. Stern, MD |
| 3/16/YR-1<br>7:15 p.m. | Satisfactory progress. Still some headache and dizziness. |
| | J. Stern, MD |
| 3/17/YR-1<br>8:00 a.m. | Discharge at 1:00 p.m. See patient as needed. Refer to private physician. |
| | J. Stern, MD |

Certified as a true and correct copy of permanent records of Memorial Hospital, Nita City, Nita.

*Sherman Fox*

---

Sherman Fox
Director, Medical Records
Memorial Hospital

**Exhibit 2**

# UNITED STATES DEPARTMENT OF THE INTERIOR
Forest Service Regional Office
Nita City, Nita 99995

July 18, YR-1

To whom it may concern:

Henry C. Fordyce was employed by this office on March 2, YR-1, when he was attending a conference on resource management at Nita City College. At the time, his job description was Senior Forest Ranger and his monthly gross salary was $7,000.

For the first month after his injury we were able to pay Mr. Fordyce because he had accumulated two weeks of sick leave and two weeks of vacation, both of which he used at that time. However, when those leaves were exhausted, we were obliged to grant Mr. Fordyce's request for personal leave without pay. For the months of April, May, and June, during which he would normally have been paid $21,000, he received no checks.

Our hospitalization plan will take care of eighty percent of all of Mr. Fordyce's bills when they are submitted for payment. According to our records, those bills have not yet been submitted.

Please do not hesitate to contact me if you have any further questions.

Sincerely,

*Richard C. Leeds*
Richard C. Leeds
Personnel Manager

RCL/pam

**Exhibit 3**

# UNITED STATES DEPARTMENT OF THE INTERIOR
Forest Service Regional Office
Nita City, Nita 99995

## MEMORANDUM

TO:        Employee File of Henry Fordyce

FROM:    T. Fleck, Supervisor    *JF*

DATE:     10/10/YR-2

RE:        Alleged Misconduct

Ranger Fordyce was accused this date of assault by Ranger Allen. Allen indicates Fordyce punched him several times after Allen said something to Fordyce about Leona Dagnit, a woman Fordyce sees socially. Allen denies provoking the fight. Fordyce says Allen implied Dagnit was immoral.

Controversy resolved internally with mutual apologies.

Exhibit 4
**Police Report of Incident**

Internal Records

| 1 AGENCY | 2 IDENTIFIER – ORI | 3 DATE | 4 OCE FILE NO |
|---|---|---|---|
| Nita City Police Dept. | NC 248/00/478 | March 2, YR-1 | 0030607746-8NC |

**5 NARRATIVE**

I was on foot patrol in vicinity of 28th Street and Founders Blvd. Was on special assignment in high crime area to show police visibility. At 11:00 p.m., received 911 report from Gus's Bar & Grill about a fight, went to premises. Entered bar, four people involved. Three men and one woman. Broke up fight. No serious injuries. Not clear who started fight. Appears two men made loud remarks concerning woman and fight ensued. Insufficient information for arrest. Took names and addresses of participants and witnesses. 11:10 p.m. sent Felson and Harris out with warning. Watched them leave in YR-3 red BMW parked 2600 block Founders. Waited at Gus's until 11:20 and resumed foot patrol.

Participants:

    Eva Marie Long, DOB 6/24/YR-26, 676 28th Street, Apt. 11B, Nita City

    Edward Felson, DOB 2/8/YR-29, Eastern Motel, Nita City

    Gerald J. Harris, DOB 7/21/YR-28, 24 Wilson Street, Glendale, Nita

    Henry C. Fordyce, DOB 8/18/YR-25, 1421 Seminole Drive, Nita City

Witnesses:

    Melissa Angel, DOB7/31/YR-27, Jackson Ave. Apt. 3B, Nita City – bartender

    James Nolan, DOB 1/6/YR-30, 14536 Davidson Pike, Nita City – cook

| 6 OFFICER'S NAME | 7 OFFICER'S SIGNATURE | 8 DATE SUBMITTED | 9 SUPERVISOR'S NAME | 10 |
|---|---|---|---|---|
| Peter C. Logan | *Peter C. Logan* | 03/05/YR-1 | Captain C. Davis | PAGE 1 OF 1 |

**Exhibit 5**
**Harris Arrest Report**

|  |  |  |  |
|---|---|---|---|
| 1 AGENCY | Nita City P.D. | 2 AGENCY IDENTIFIER NO. | 439/45/789 |
| 3 OCA FILE NO. | 2126-03-06354-89 | COURT STATUS — 4 PENDING / 5 COMPLETE | XXX |

**DISPOSITION**

| 55 DATE | 56 COURT DOCKET |
|---|---|
| 3/19/YR-1 | NO. CR-3-586 |

| 6 NAME – LAST | FIRST | MIDDLE | 7 ALIAS – NICKNAME |
|---|---|---|---|
| Harris | Gerald | J. | n/a |

57 COURT: Nita County District Court, Galloway, Judge

| 8 COMPLETE ADDRESS | 9 PLACE OF BIRTH |
|---|---|
| 24 Wilson Street, Glendale, Nita | Nita City, Nita |

| 10 RACE | 11 SEX | 12 AGE | 13 DATE OF BIRTH | 14 HEIGHT | 15 WEIGHT | 16 HAIR | 17 EYES |
|---|---|---|---|---|---|---|---|
| c. | M | 27 | 7/21/YR-28 | 6' | 175 | Brown | Hazel |

58 AS CHARGED    59 LESSER

| 18 COMPLEXION | 19 MARRIED | 20 OTHER DESCRIPTIVE INFORMATION |
|---|---|---|
| Light | No | |

60 DISMISSED: XXX    61 ACQUITTED

| 21 PRINTS TAKEN | 22 PHOTOGRAPH TAKEN | 23 SOC. SEC. NO. | 24 DRIVER LICENSE NO. |
|---|---|---|---|
| Yes | Yes | 044-89-1184 | Nita 3836589 |

62 SENTENCE

| 25 EMPLOYER – SCHOOL | 26 OCCUPATION | 27 ADDRESS |
|---|---|---|
| Sanders Cleaning | Owner | 2608 Founders Blvd., Nita City, Nita |

**DETAILS OF ARREST**

| 28 DATE ARRESTED | 29 TIME | 30 PLACE ARRESTED | 32 UCR CODE |
|---|---|---|---|
| 3/5/YR-1 | 2:00 p.m. | Place of business | 045 |

31 CHARGE(S): Assault with a deadly weapon

33 COMPLAINANT'S NAME AND ADDRESS: Henry Fordyce, 1421 Seminole Drive, Nita City, Nita

| 34 WITH WARRANT | 35 W/O WARRANT | 36 ON VIEW | 37 SUMMONS | 38 JUVENILE | 39 DISP. OF JUVENILE |
|---|---|---|---|---|---|
| | XXX | | | | |

| 40 DATE OF OFFENSE | 41 TIME | 42 LOCATION OF OFFENSE |
|---|---|---|
| 3/2/YR-1 | 11:30 p.m. | 27th block of Founders Blvd., Nita City, Nita |

| 43 VEHICLE INFORMATION (YEAR, MAKE, BODY TYPE, COLOR, LIC NO & STATE) | 44 PLACE VEHICLE STORED |
|---|---|
| n/a | n/a |

63 OTHER – DESCRIBE

**BAIL INFORMATION**

| 45 DATE | 46 COURT | (MAGISTRATE/JUDGE) | 47 TRIAL DATE |
|---|---|---|---|
| 3/5/YR-1 | District Court | Galloway | 3/19/YR-1 |

| 48 AMOUNT BAIL | 49 HELD ON BAIL | 50 ROR | 51 COMMITTED | 52 COMMITTED W/O BAIL | 53 PLACE COMMITTED |
|---|---|---|---|---|---|
| $5,0000 | XXX | | | | |

64 RIGHT THUMB

**54 NARRATIVE**

At 11:35 p.m. heard screaming and returned to vicinity of 2847 Founders Blvd. Gus's Bar where previous incident occurred (see earlier report dated 3/2/YR-1). Saw subject, female, running toward me yelling, "He is killing my friend." Subject, Eva Marie Long, DOB 6.24.YR-26 had been involved in earlier incident at same location. I ran to location indicated by her – an alley between 27th and 28th Sts. On Founders Blvd. Found second subject involved in earlier fight same location.

| 65 OFFICER'S NAME | 66 SIGNATURE | 67 DATE | 68 SUPERVISOR'S SIGNATURE | 69 RECORDED | 70 ARRESTEE'S SIGNATURE |
|---|---|---|---|---|---|
| Peter C. Logan | Peter C. Logan | 3/5/YR-1 | Captain C. Davis | 3/19/YR-1 | Gerald Harris |

Internal Records

| 1 AGENCY | 2 IDENTIFIER – ORI | 3 CONFIGURATION TO | 4 OCE FILE NO |
|---|---|---|---|
| Nita City Police Dept. | NC 439/45/789 | ☐ INVESTIGATION<br>☐ SUPPLEMENTARY INV. | 2126-03-06354-89 |

**5 NARRATIVE**

Henry C. Fordyce, DOB 8/18/YR-25, unconscious on sidewalk. Bleeding from head, nose, and ears, called for ambulance and backup. Long and Fordyce went to hospital in ambulance. I followed in watch commander's vehicle. At hospital Long immediately informed me that attackers in second fight were same as in earlier fight. Had notes from earlier investigation. Put out BOLO on Edward Felson, DOB 2/8/YR-29, and Gerald J. Harris, DOB 7/21/YR-28.

3/5/YR-1: Detectives brought in suspects Harris and Felson. Both arrested this date. Suspects given rights and placed in lineup. Seven men involved. Long originally identifies both Felson and Harris. Further questioning by detectives indicates, not positive suspect Felson present at time of assault. Witness now not sure two assailants were present in alley at time of assault. Will make weak witness. Victim still hospitalized, unable to participate in lineup. Bond set at $5,000 for both suspects. Suspect Harris released on bond. Suspect Felson detained.

3/6/YR-1: Investigation reveals no additional witnesses to alleged crime. Suspects make no statements on advice of counsel. At arraignment, this date, confirmed by Asst. District Attorney that cases won't stick.

3/19/YR-1: Case against both suspects dismissed. Suspect Felson released.

| 6 OFFICER'S NAME | 7 OFFICER'S SIGNATURE | 8 DATE SUBMITTED | 9 SUPERVISOR'S NAME | 10 |
|---|---|---|---|---|
| Peter C. Logan | *Peter C. Logan* | 03/19/YR-1 | Captain C. Davis | PAGE 2 OF 2 |

National Institute for Trial Advocacy

**Exhibit 5 (3)**
**Street Diagram**

28th Street

Coffee
Shop

Electronics
Store

Women's
Clothing
Store

Alley          **X**

Vacant
Store

Gus's Bar
& Grill

Ice Cream

Sidewalk

27th Street

Founders
Boulevard

N

Legend:

◯     Street Light

**X**     Victim Found

**Prepared by Off. Peter C. Logan, 3/5/YR-1**

Exhibit 6
Felson Arrest Report

|  |  |  |
|---|---|---|
| 1 | AGENCY | Nita City P.D. |
| 2 | AGENCY IDENTIFIER NO. | 439/45/789 |
| 3 | OCA FILE NO. | 2126-03-06354-89 |
| | COURT STATUS | |
| 4 | PENDING | |
| 5 | COMPLETE | XXX |
| | DISPOSITION | |
| 55 | DATE | 3/19/YR-1 |
| 56 | COURT DOCKET NO. | CR-3-587 |
| 6 | NAME – LAST | Felson |
| | FIRST | Edward |
| | MIDDLE | W. |
| 7 | ALIAS – NICKNAME | n/a |
| 57 | COURT | Nita County District Court Galloway, Judge |
| 8 | COMPLETE ADDRESS | Eastern Motel, Nita City, Nita |
| 9 | PLACE OF BIRTH | Nita City, Nita |
| 10 | RACE | c. |
| 11 | SEX | M |
| 12 | AGE | 29 |
| 13 | DATE OF BIRTH | 2/8/YR-29 |
| 14 | HEIGHT | 5'11" |
| 15 | WEIGHT | 165 |
| 16 | HAIR | Brown |
| 17 | EYES | Brown |
| 58 | AS CHARGED | |
| 59 | LESSER | |
| 18 | COMPLEXION | Dark |
| 19 | MARRIED | No |
| 20 | OTHER DESCRIPTIVE INFORMATION | |
| 21 | PRINTS TAKEN | Yes |
| 22 | PHOTOGRAPH TAKEN | Yes |
| 23 | SOC. SEC. NO. | 147-28-9183 |
| 24 | DRIVER LICENSE NO. | Nita 4934143 |
| 60 | DISMISSED | XXX |
| 61 | ACQUITTED | |
| 25 | EMPLOYER – SCHOOL | unemployed |
| 26 | OCCUPATION | n/a |
| 27 | ADDRESS | n/a |
| 62 | SENTENCE | |
| | DETAILS OF ARREST | |
| 28 | DATE ARRESTED | 3/5/YR-1 |
| 29 | TIME | 12:45 p.m. |
| 30 | PLACE ARRESTED | Residence |
| 31 | CHARGE(S) | Assault with a deadly weapon |
| 32 | UCR CODE | 045 |
| 33 | COMPLAINANT'S NAME AND ADDRESS | Henry Fordyce, 1421 Seminole Drive, Nita City, Nita |
| 34 | WITH WARRANT | XXX |
| 35 | W/O WARRANT | XXX |
| 36 | ON VIEW | |
| 37 | SUMMONS | |
| 38 | JUVENILE | |
| 39 | DISP. OF JUVENILE | |
| 40 | DATE OF OFFENSE | 3/2/YR-1 |
| 41 | TIME | 11:30 p.m. |
| 42 | LOCATION OF OFFENSE | 27th block of Founders Blvd., Nita City, Nita |
| 43 | VEHICLE INFORMATION (YEAR, MAKE, BODY TYPE, COLOR, LIC NO & STATE) | n/a |
| 44 | PLACE VEHICLE STORED | n/a |
| 63 | OTHER – DESCRIBE | |
| | BAIL INFORMATION | |
| 45 | DATE | 3/5/YR-1 |
| 46 | COURT | District Court |
| | (MAGISTRATE/JUDGE) | Galloway |
| 47 | TRIAL DATE | 3/19/YR-1 |
| 48 | AMOUNT BAIL | $5,0000 |
| 49 | HELD ON BAIL | XXX |
| 50 | ROR | |
| 51 | COMMITTED | |
| 52 | COMMITTED W/O BAIL | |
| 53 | PLACE COMMITTED | Nita City Jail |
| 54 | NARRATIVE | See attached report for Gerald J. Harris, co-defendant. |
| 64 | RIGHT THUMB | |
| 65 | OFFICER'S NAME | Peter C. Logan |
| 66 | SIGNATURE | Peter C. Logan |
| 67 | DATE | 3/5/YR-1 |
| 68 | SUPERVISOR'S SIGNATURE | Captain C. Davis |
| 69 | RECORDED | 3/19/YR-1 |
| 70 | ARRESTEE'S SIGNATURE | Edward W. Felson |

Exhibit 7
Floor Layout of Gus's Bar & Grill

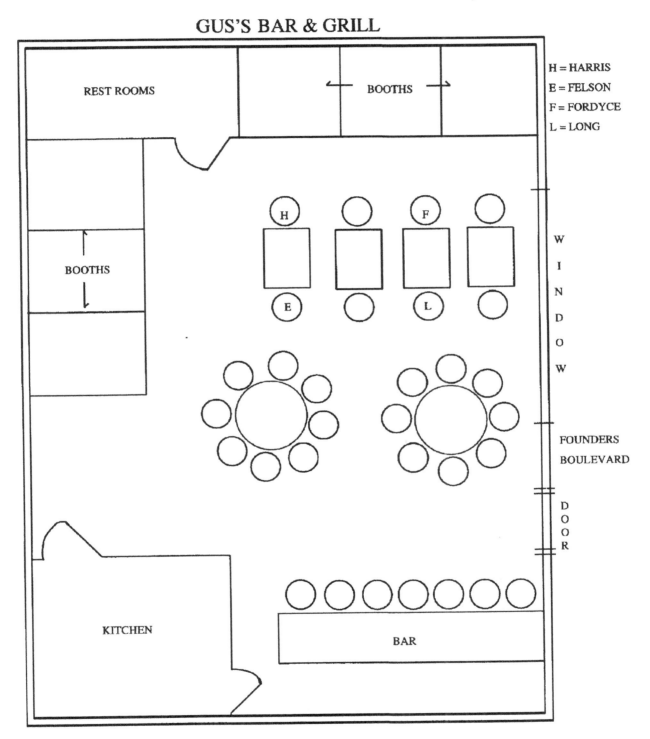

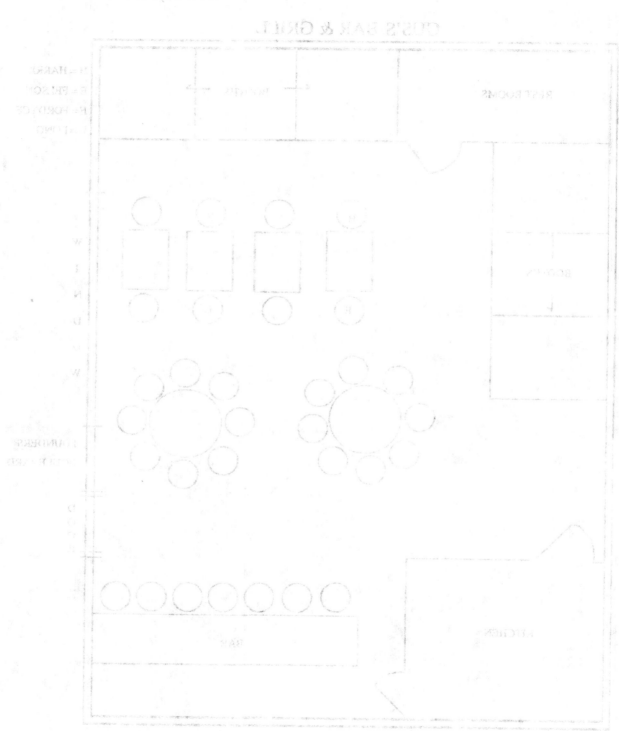

Exhibit 8
Nita City Streets

| | | | | | | | | |
|---|---|---|---|---|---|---|---|---|
| 30th | | | | | | | | |
| 29th | | | | | | | | |
| 28th x | Arena | Long x | | | | | | |
| 27th | | Gus's x | | | | | | |
| 26th | | | x Sander's Cleaning | | | | | |
| 25th | | | | | | | | |
| 24th | | | | | | | | |
| 23rd | | | | | | | | |
| 22nd | | | | | | | | |
| 21st | | | | | | | | |
| 20th | | | | | | | | |
| 19th | | | | | | | | |
| 18th | | | | | | | | |
| 17th | | | | | | | | |
| 16th | | | | | | | | |
| 15th | | | | | | | | |
| 14th | | | | | | | | |
| 13th | | | | | | | | |
| 12th | | | | | | | | |
| 11th | | | | | | | | |
| 10th | | | | | | | | |
| 9th | | | | | | | | |
| 8th | | | | | | | | |
| 7th | | | | | | | | |
| 6th | | | | | | | | |
| 5th | | x Barkan | | | | | | |
| 4th | | | | | | | | |
| 3rd | | | | | | | | |
| 2nd | | | | | | | | |
| 1st | | | | | | | | |

N ↑

→

To
Eastern
Motel
(.5 mile)

Jackson Avenue
Indiana Avenue
Holt Avenue
Grace Avenue
Founders Boulevard
Edison Concourse
Davidson Pike
Corona Avenue
Boulder Avenue

To Glendale
(15 miles) ↓

**Exhibit 9**

## UNIFORM ARREST AND DISPOSITION RECORD

| NAME: | Henry C. Fordyce | DOB: | 8/18/YR-25 |
|-------|------------------|------|------------|
| S.S. NO: | 037-46-5756 | POB: | Nita City, Nita |

| DATE | ADDRESS | OFFENSE | DISPOSITION |
|------|---------|---------|-------------|
| 3/8/YR-3 | RFD Rt 27 Wolf Creek, Nita | Drunk and disorderly | Dismissed |
| 1/1/YR-3 | RFD Rt 27 Wolf Creek, Nita | Drunk and disorderly; Assault on a Police Officer | Dismissed |

*Alexander McConachie*

Alexander McConachie
Superintendent of Documents

Certified as of this 1st day of October, YR-1.

*Charlotte Noll*

Charlotte Noll
Notary Public

**Exhibit 10**

## UNIFORM ARREST AND DISPOSITION RECORD

| NAME: | Eva Marie Long | DOB: | 6/24/YR-26 |
|---|---|---|---|
| S.S. NO: | 288-27-4414 | POB: | Racine, WI |

| DATE | ADDRESS | OFFENSE | DISPOSITION |
|---|---|---|---|
| 1/17/YR-2 | 676 28th St. Nita City, Nita | Poss. w/int Cocaine (felony) | Dismissed |
| 7/30/YR-2 | 676 28th St Nita City, Nita | Poss. w/int Cocaine (felony) | Dismissed |

*Alexander McConachie*

Alexander McConachie
Superintendent of Documents

Certified as of this 1st day of October, YR-1.

*Charlotte Noll*

Charlotte Noll
Notary Public

**Exhibit 11**

## UNIFORM ARREST AND DISPOSITION RECORD

| NAME: | Gerald J. Harris | DOB: | 7/21/YR-28 |
|---|---|---|---|
| S.S. NO: | 044-89-1184 | POB: | Nita City, Nita |

| DATE | ADDRESS | OFFENSE | DISPOSITION |
|---|---|---|---|
| 10/12/YR-14 | 4727 Holt Ave. Nita City, Nita | Purse Snatching | Released to custody of parents |
| 12/3/YR-14 | 4727 Holt Ave. Nita City, Nita | Assault | Released to custody of parents |
| 6/24/YR-13 | 4727 Holt Ave. Nita City, Nita | Assault | Adj. delinquent 1 yr. probation |
| 8/12/YR-12 | 4727 Holt Ave. Nita City, Nita | Carrying Concealed Weapon | Adj. delinquent 2 yrs. probation |
| 4/28/YR-11 | 4727 Holt Ave. Nita City, Nita | Assault w/Deadly Weapon | Probation violation, 1 yr. Training School Released 12/20/YR-11 |
| 3/5/YR-1 | 4 Wilson St. Glendale, Nita | Assault w/Deadly Weapon | Dismissed |

*Alexander McConachie*

Alexander McConachie
Superintendent of Documents

Certified as of this 1st day of October, YR-1.

*Charlotte Noll*

Charlotte Noll
Notary Public

**Exhibit 12**

## UNIFORM ARREST AND DISPOSITION RECORD

| NAME: | Edward W. Felson | DOB: | 2/8/YR-29 |
|---|---|---|---|
| S.S. NO: | 147-28-9183 | POB: | Hartford, Nita |

| DATE | ADDRESS | OFFENSE | DISPOSITION |
|---|---|---|---|
| 1/12/YR-6 | 1020 N. Broad St. Philadelphia, PA | Disorderly Conduct (Misdeameanor) | G/P $25.00 fine |
| 8/14/YR-4 | 9529 Kenyon Ave. Nita City, Nita | Larceny/auto theft (felony) | Jury Trial Guilty/6 mos. State Prison |
| 10/21/YR-3 | 9529 Kenyon Ave. Nita City, Nita | Assault (felony) | Dismissed |
| 3/5/YR-1 | Eastern Motel Nita City, Nita | Assault w/Deadly Weapon | Dismissed |
| 7/10/YR-1 | Eastern Motel Nita City, Nita | Armed Robbery (felony) | Pending |

*Alexander McConachie*

Alexander McConachie
Superintendent of Documents

Certified as of this lst day of October, YR-1.

*Charlotte Noll*

Charlotte Noll
Notary Public

## UNIFORM ARREST AND DISPOSITION RECORD

| NAME | Drug W. Phenn | DOB | 7-9-18-29 |
|---|---|---|---|
| SS | 1372-25-9154 | POB | Hartford, Nita |

| DATE | ADDRESS | OFFENSE | DISPOSITION |
|---|---|---|---|
| | 1920 N. Broad St., Philadelphia, PA | Disorderly Conduct (misdemeanor) | O/R $25.00 fine |
| | 1220 Kenyon Ave., Nita City, Nita | Larceny, auto theft (felony) | Jury Trial — Guilty, State Prison |
| | Kaufman Ave., Nita City, Nita | Assault (felony) | Dismissed |
| | Eastern Motel, Nita City, Nita | Assault with Deadly Weapon | Dismissed |
| | Eastern Motel, Nita City, Nita | Armed Robbery (felony) | Pending |

Alexander MacClain
Superintendent of Documents

Charlotte Holt
Notary Public

**Exhibit 13**

# MEMORIAL HOSPITAL
## NITA CITY, NITA 99997

PATIENT:   Eva Marie Long
           676 28th St.
           Nita City, Nita

DOB:        June 24, YR-26

NOK:        Mr. Joseph M. Long
            2417 Pinecrest Drive
            Montrose, Nita

EMPLOYER: Self-employed

INSURANCE: None                    ADMITTED:  9/2/YR-1 1:05 a.m.

9/2/YR-1
1:05 a.m.
ER Patient brought in by friend who declined to give name. Friend reports victim had been using cocaine. Ordered blood and urine samples stat. Observation of depressed respiration, pulse, and B.P. Reports confirm initial diagnosis of cocaine overdose. Patient improved rapidly. Hospitalization not necessary. Released at 10:00 a.m. with instructions to return in the event of any future problems.

B. Chakabarty, MD

Certified as a true and correct copy of permanent records of Memorial Hospital, Nita City, Nita.

*Sherman Fox*

Sherman Fox
Director, Medical Records
Memorial Hospital

# CONFIDENTIAL REPORT

Prepared for:    State's Attorney

Prepared by:    David Peterson, Nita Investigations, Inc.

Date:   October 20, YR-1

Pursuant to your request, our office has investigated Gerald Harris's business, Sanders Cleaning Service, Inc., regarding possible overcharges on contracts with Nita City.

Our investigation reveals that Sanders had the contract for cleaning with the Nita City Department of Housing, which is located at 27 Smith Street. This contract commenced on July 1, YR-2, and was for a maximum term of three years. Each party had the option to renew for each year during the term. On June 1, YR-1, the Housing Authority wrote Mr. Harris, informing him that the contract would not be renewed and would instead terminate on June 30, YR-1. The letter did not give any reasons. Our informant in that office indicates that the Department of Housing believed they had been charged substantial sums for work that had not been performed.

On August 18, YR-1, the Department of Housing brought suit in Nita County Superior Court seeking repayment of $27,000 in alleged overcharges. The action was dismissed with prejudice on September 2, YR-1. Our informant further indicates that a settlement led to the dismissal and that, as a result of the settlement, Sanders Cleaning Services, Inc., paid the department $10,000.

Please do not hesitate to contact us if we can be of further assistance.

# STATEMENT OF BEN SANDERS*
## FEBRUARY 15, YR-0

My name is Ben Sanders, and I live at 1253 Melville Road, Glendale, Nita. I am sixty-eight years old and retired. I have been married to Alice Sanders for forty-seven years. We have three children and five grandchildren.

I have known Gerry Harris since he and my youngest son went to grade school together. My son Billy and Gerry were friends then, although they later went to different junior high schools. Gerry began to hang out with the wrong crowd and got into trouble. I coached my son's baseball team and needed a catcher, and I knew Gerry could play, so I asked him to play on my son's team. Maybe I could help turn him around. I think it helped.

After high school, Gerry came to work for me. He quickly learned the business and became very knowledgeable about the whole operation—hiring, finances, customer relations, contracts. My own sons never wanted to learn the business, so Gerry became my "business" son. After a few years, Gerry approached me to buy the business. At first I was concerned, because this business is based on personal contacts, reputation, and goodwill, but Gerry had proven himself. As I was looking to retire, I agreed to sell it to him in YR-3. He pays me yearly out of net earnings. He currently owes $225,000 on the note.

In my contacts with Gerry, I have known him to be a fine man not easily angered or inclined to use profanity. He has been in situations where another man might have lost his temper, but he didn't. He also does not drink to excess. I have never seen him drunk in any business or personal situation. He has a steady girlfriend, Glenda Barkan, and they come to our house for dinner often. I think they will marry soon.

I know he was arrested for a fight a Gus's Bar, but I know he didn't start it. Gus's is a little rough-and-tumble place near the office. Eddie Felson was there, and it is more likely that Felson was involved. He was a violent kid in high school.

Gerry would never have ambushed the guy outside the bar. He is not that kind of person. In my community, he has the reputation of being honest, law-abiding, and even-tempered. I know because I asked around.

*Ben Sanders*

_____

Ben Sanders

_____

\* This statement was given to the defense attorney and provided to the State's Attorney by defense counsel.

# Jury Instructions

## 1. Nita Preliminary Instruction 01:01 Introduction

You have been selected as jurors and have taken an oath to well and truly try this cause. This trial will last one day.

During the progress of the trial, there will be periods of time when the Court recesses. During those periods of time, you must not talk about this case among yourselves or with anyone else.

During the trial, do not talk to any of the parties, their lawyers, or any of the witnesses.

If any attempt is made by anyone to talk to you concerning the matters here under consideration, you should immediately report that fact to the Court.

You should keep an open mind. You should not form or express an opinion during the trial and should reach no conclusion in this case until you have heard all of the evidence, the arguments of counsel, and the final instructions as to the law that will be given to you by the Court.

## 2. Nita Preliminary Instruction 01:02 Conduct of the Trial

First, the attorneys will have an opportunity to make opening statements. These statements are not evidence and should be considered only as a preview of what the attorneys expect the evidence will be.

Following the opening statements, witnesses will be called to testify. They will be placed under oath and questioned by the attorneys. Documents and other tangible exhibits may also be received as evidence. If an exhibit is given to you to examine, you should examine it carefully, individually, and without any comment.

It is counsel's right and duty to object when testimony or other evidence is being offered that he or she believes is not admissible.

When the Court sustains an objection to a question, the jurors must disregard the question and the answer, if one has been given, and draw no inference from the question or answer or speculate as to what the witness would have said if permitted to answer. Jurors must also disregard evidence stricken from the record.

When the Court sustains an objection to any evidence the jurors must disregard that evidence.

When the Court overrules an objection to any evidence, the jurors must not give that evidence any more weight than if the objection had not been made.

When the evidence is completed, the attorneys will make closing arguments. These final statements are not evidence, but are given to assist you in evaluating the evidence. The attorneys are also permitted to argue in an attempt to persuade you to a particular verdict. You may accept or reject those arguments as you see fit.

Finally, just before you retire to consider your verdict, the Court will give you further instructions on the law that applies to this case.

# PART II
# FINAL INSTRUCTIONS

## 3. Nita Instruction 1:01 Introduction

Members of the jury, the evidence and arguments in this case have been completed, and I will now instruct you as to the law.

The law applicable to this case is stated in these instructions, and it is your duty to follow all of them. You must not single out certain instructions and disregard others.

It is your duty to determine the facts and to determine them only from the evidence in this case. You are to apply the law to the facts and in this way decide the case. You must not be governed or influenced by sympathy or prejudice for or against any party in this case. Your verdict must be based on evidence and not on speculation, guess, or conjecture.

From time to time the court has ruled on the admissibility of evidence. You must not concern yourselves with the reasons for these rulings. You should disregard questions and exhibits that were withdrawn or to which objections were sustained.

You should also disregard testimony and exhibits that the court has refused or stricken.

The evidence that you should consider consists only of the witnesses' testimonies and the exhibits the court has received.

Any evidence that was received for a limited purpose should not be considered by you for any other purpose.

You should consider all the evidence in the light of your own observations and experiences in life.

Neither by these instructions nor by any ruling or remark that I have made do I mean to indicate any opinion as to the facts or as to what your verdict should be.

## 4. Nita Instruction 1:02 Opening Statements and Closing Arguments

Opening statements are made by the attorneys to acquaint you with the facts they expect to prove. Closing arguments are made by the attorneys to discuss the facts and circumstances in the case, and should be confined to the evidence and to reasonable inferences to be drawn from it. Neither opening statements nor closing arguments are evidence, and any statement or argument made by the attorneys that is not based on the evidence should be disregarded.

## 5. Nita Instruction 1:03 Credibility of Witnesses

You are the sole judges of the credibility of the witnesses and of the weight to be given to the testimony of each witness. In determining what credit is to be given any witness, you may take into account his ability and opportunity to observe; his manner and appearance while testifying; any interest, bias, or prejudice he may have; the reasonableness of his testimony considered in the light of all the evidence; and any other factors that bear on the believability and weight of the witness's testimony.

## 6. Nita Instruction 1:05 Direct and Circumstantial Evidence

The law recognizes two kinds of evidence: direct and circumstantial. Direct evidence proves a fact directly; that is, the evidence by itself, if true, establishes the fact. Circumstantial evidence is the proof of facts or circumstances that give rise to a reasonable inference of other facts; that is, circumstantial evidence proves a fact indirectly in that it follows from other facts or circumstances according to common experience and observations in life. An eyewitness is a common example of direct evidence, while human footprints are circumstantial evidence that a person was present.

The law makes no distinction between direct and circumstantial evidence as to the degree or amount of proof required, and each should be considered according to whatever weight or value it may have. All of the evidence should be considered and evaluated by you in arriving at your verdict.

## 7. Nita Instruction 3:01 Indictment

The indictment in this case is the formal method of accusing the defendant of a crime and placing him on trial. It is not any evidence against the defendant and does not create any inference of guilt. The State has the burden of proving beyond a reasonable doubt every essential element of the crime charged in the indictment (or any of the crimes included therein).

## 8. Nita Instruction 3:02 Burden of Proof

The State has the burden of proving the guilt of the defendant beyond a reasonable doubt, and this burden remains on the State throughout the case. The defendant is not required to prove his innocence.

## 9. Nita Instruction 3:03 Reasonable Doubt

Reasonable doubt means a doubt based on reason and common sense that arises from a fair and rational consideration of all the evidence or lack of evidence in the case. It is a doubt that is not a vague, speculative, or imaginary doubt, but such a doubt as would cause reasonable persons to hesitate to act in matters of importance to themselves.

## 10. Nita Instruction 3:04 Presumption of Innocence

The defendant is presumed to be innocent of the charges against him. This presumption remains with him throughout every stage of the trial and during your deliberations on the verdict. The presumption is not overcome until, from all the evidence in the case, you are convinced beyond a reasonable doubt that the defendant is guilty.

**11.** The State of Nita has charged the defendant with the crime of First Degree Assault with a Deadly Weapon, which includes the crimes of Second Degree Assault Causing Serious Bodily Injury and Third Degree Assault.

**12.** A lesser included offense is an offense that includes some but not all of the elements present in the crime charged. If you find from a consideration of all the evidence that the defendant did not commit the crime charged, you may consider whether or not the defendant committed one of the lesser included offenses.

**13.** To find the defendant guilty of the crime charged or any of the lesser included offenses, the State of Nita has the burden of proving the elements of the offense beyond a reasonable doubt. A reasonable doubt is a fair and actual doubt. It is not a doubt based on imagination or speculation.

**14.** In determining the issues in this case, you should be guided by the following definitions:

**Deadly Weapon** means any firearm, knife, bludgeon, or other weapon, device, instrument, material, or substance that in the manner it is used is capable of producing death or serious bodily injury.

**Serious Bodily Injury** means bodily injury that involves a substantial risk of death, serious permanent disfigurement, or longstanding loss or impairment of the function of any part or organ of the body.

**Bodily Injury** means physical pain, illness, or impairment of physical or mental condition.

**15.** The first charge you must consider is first degree assault with a deadly weapon. In order to find the defendant guilty, you must find that the defendant Gerald Harris, in the State of Nita, on or about March 2, YR-1 with intent to cause serious bodily injury to another person, caused serious bodily injury to Henry Fordyce, by means of a deadly weapon. If you find that each of these elements has been proved beyond a reasonable doubt, then you shall find the defendant guilty. If you find that one or more of these elements have not been proved beyond a reasonable doubt, then you shall consider the charge of second degree assault causing serious bodily injury.

**16.** In order to find the defendant guilty of second degree assault causing serious bodily injury, you must find that the defendant Gerald Harris, in the State of Nita, on or about March 2, YR-1 with intent to cause serious bodily injury to another person, caused serious bodily injury to Henry Fordyce. If you find that one or more of these elements have not been proved beyond a reasonable doubt, then you shall consider the charge of third degree assault causing bodily injury.

**17.** In order to find he defendant guilty of third degree assault causing bodily injury, you must find that the defendant Gerald Harris, in the State of Nita, on or about March 2, YR-1 with intent to cause bodily injury to another person, caused bodily injury to Henry Fordyce. If you find that one or more of these elements have not been proved beyond a reasonable doubt, then you shall find the defendant not guilty.

**18. Nita Instruction 3:05 Reputation/Character**

The defendant has introduced evidence of his character and reputation for (truth and veracity) (being a peaceful and law abiding citizen) (morality) (chastity) (honesty and integrity) (etc.). This evidence may be sufficient when considered with the other evidence in the case to raise a reasonable doubt of the defendant's guilt. However, if from all the evidence in the case you are satisfied beyond a reasonable doubt of the defendant's guilt, then it is your duty to find him guilty, even though he may have a good reputation for (truth and veracity) (being a peaceful and law abiding citizen) (morality) (chastity) (honesty and integrity) (etc.).

**19.** The Defendant has offered the defense of alibi. This is a real defense, which if accepted must result in the Defendant's acquittal. Alibi means that at the time of the crime, the Defendant was at another place. Defendant has the burden of proving this alibi defense by a preponderance of the evidence, meaning the greater weight of the evidence.

## 20. Nita Instruction 1:06 Concluding Instruction

The Court did not in any way and does not by these instructions give or intimate any opinions as to what has or has not been proven in the case, or as to what are or are not the facts of the case.

No one of these instructions states all of the law applicable, but all of them must be taken, read, and considered together as they are connected with and related to each other as a whole.

You must not be concerned with the wisdom of any rule of law. Regardless of any opinions you may have as to what the law ought to be, it would be a violation of your sworn duty to base a verdict on any other view of the law than that given in the instructions of the Court.

## In the District Court
## of the County of Darrow
## State of Nita

| | | |
|---|---|---|
| STATE OF NITA | ) | |
| | ) | |
| v. | ) | JURY VERDICT |
| | ) | |
| GERALD HARRIS | ) | |

## YOU ARE TO SIGN AND RETURN ONLY ONE VERDICT

## I. NOT GUILTY

We, the Jury, find the Defendant, Gerald Harris, NOT GUILTY.

_____
Foreperson

## II. FIRST DEGREE ASSAULT WITH A DEADLY WEAPON

We, the Jury, find the Defendant, Gerald Harris, GUILTY of First Degree Assault with a Deadly Weapon.

_____
Foreperson

## III. SECOND DEGREE ASSAULT CAUSING SERIOUS BODILY INJURY

We, the Jury, find the Defendant, Gerald Harris, GUILTY of Second Degree Assault causing Serious Bodily Injury.

_____
Foreperson

## IV. THIRD DEGREE ASSAULT

We, the Jury, find the Defendant, Gerald Harris, GUILTY of Third Degree Assault.

_____
Foreperson